# First Tears

### over the Loss of Your Child

Linda Anderson

## acta
PUBLICATIONS

**First Tears over the Loss of Your Child**
by Linda Anderson

Edited by Andrew Yankech
Cover design by Tom A. Wright
Text design and typesetting by Patricia A. Lynch

Scripture quotes are from the *New Revised Standard Version of the Bible*, copyright © 1989 by the Division of Christian Education of the National Council of the Churches of Christ in the USA. All rights reserved. Used with permission.

Every effort was made to ensure that proper permission and credit were obtained and given for copyrighted material. Any error or omission is inadvertent and will be corrected in future editions.

Published by ACTA Publications, 5559 W. Howard Street, Skokie, IL 60077-2621, (800) 397-2282, www.actapublications.com

Library of Congress Number: 2008942253
ISBN: 978-0-87946-379-3
Printed in The United States by Evangel Press
Year 16 15 14 13 12 11 10 09
Printing 10 09 08 07 06 05 04 03 02 First Edition

# Contents

In loving memory of my daughter
Sally Elizabeth Anderson, 1970-1995

Welcome

n July 24, 1995, my youngest daughter took her own life. She was twenty-five years old. Her death was incomprehensible to those who knew and loved her.

When Sally died, our friends and our community asked themselves, "How could that have happened to *her*? Didn't her family love her enough? Didn't she realize her talents? Didn't she know how devastating her death would be to those who loved her?"

My husband and I had no experience with suicide, nor did we know anyone whose child had died in that manner. We were totally unprepared for the long journey we had to make.

We were given several books about grieving and we were grateful for the thoughtfulness of those who sent them. Each of the books had merit, but merely reading other people's stories was not enough to lift us out of our sorrow. I kept asking myself, "How can I go from where I am to living a meaningful life again?"

Over time, I came to understand that parents who have lost a child need more than other people's stories. They need to realize that they are not alone. They need hope that things will get better. They need to be able to move forward, renew their spirits, and understand the steps they will likely take on their own grief walk. Most of all, however, bereaved parents need to feel loved.

This volume offers commiseration, hope, renewal, understanding and love to anyone who has lost a child.

My hope is that these pages will help you to reach out to others, to share your sorrow, and to heal. I also hope this book will be of value to your friends and family who may not understand what you are feeling, or how to best support you in your grief. May this book help them to be a loving and comforting presence in your life.

*Linda Anderson*

First
Tears

child's death is not part of the natural cycle of life. It is unexpected and incomprehensible.

When the chain of order is dissolved and our child dies, we lose something of ourselves. There is a special bond between parents and their children that includes nurturing, protecting, comforting, supporting, encouraging, loving, and accepting them. It is no wonder our world is turned upside down when a child dies.

You and I have singular stories to tell, but we are alike in the pain that we feel. We grieve differently, but our need for affirmation is the same.

The "why" is unanswerable, but we can help each other by acknowledging our common sorrow and then encouraging each other to step back into life. We must accept our emotions as well as our loss.

When we feel physical pain, we know that it can intensify if we ignore it. Pain is our body's way of telling us something is wrong, and we can learn from it. So too can we learn from emotional pain. To fully grieve and heal, we need to open ourselves to our pain and our loss. We also need to allow ourselves plenty of time for the grieving process.

It has been said that when you lose a child, you lose the future. But that is not true. Your future is being changed into the present with every passing moment, and how we decide to live our lives will decide our future.

Many corporate employee benefits offer a set number of bereavement days after the death of a family member, as if our grief could possibly be contained in a definite amount of time. Friends and colleagues may expect us to quickly get over our loss and get on with life, but there is no time limit to grief. It comes and goes throughout our lives, changed and blunted with the passage of time, but always there.

We never get over missing our child. Yet by reconciling ourselves to our loss, we can allow happiness to grow around the memories of our loved ones.

Tears do not flow only from
the pitiful and the weak.
They spring also from the love and
tenderness of the strong.
We should never be ashamed of our tears,
whether in private sorrow or public grieving.
Tears alleviate our grief
and encourage
the healing of our wounds.

*Anonymous*

Give voice to sorrow,
and words to loneliness,
make heard the depth of your despair
and the breaking of your heart.
For what remains unspoken
can never burst into healing song.

*Molly Fumie*

When we have accepted the worst,
we have nothing more to lose.
That automatically means
we have everything to gain.

*Dale Carnegie*

And
through
all the tears
and the sadness
and the pain
comes the one thought
that can make me
internally
smile again:
I
have
loved.

*Patti Jo Foye*

Sadness needs its own time to be.

*Karen Berry*

You gain strength,
courage,
and confidence
by every experience
in which you
really stop
to look
loss
in the face.

*Eleanor Roosevelt*

Heartbreak is Life educating us.

*George Bernard Shaw*

When someone dies, and you're not expecting it, you don't
lose them all at once; you lose them in pieces over a long
time—the way mail stops coming, and the scent fades
from the pillows and clothes.

*From* A Prayer for Owen Meany
*by John Irving*

The hilltop would not be half so wonderful
if there were no dark valleys to traverse.

*Helen Keller*

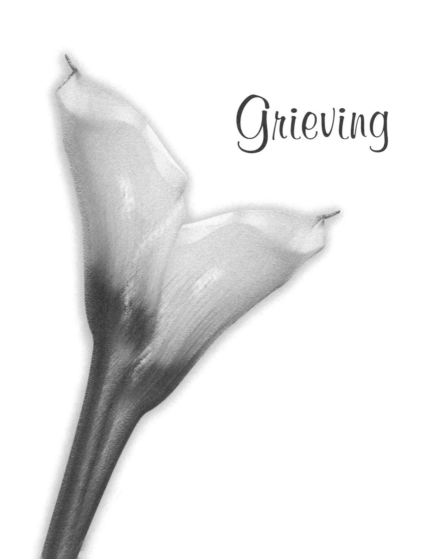

Grieving

here are days when we have to draw out the strength to function from somewhere deep inside us. Even though we may feel like we cannot do it, somehow we manage.

In our culture, it is a virtue to be strong. But denial is not a form of strength. Expressions such as "keep a stiff upper lip," "get a hold of yourself," or "it's time to move on," do not help those who are mourning. They exhort us to hide our grief and continue with life before we are ready. Instead, we need to take as long as necessary to heal. Statements like "I'll be here for you," "I don't mind if you cry," and "I'll be glad to listen," are compassionate and realistic expressions. When people offer us love and support they become sources of strength.

Having the courage to grieve and accept the death of your child means examining your life and your values so that you can recreate a life of purpose and find the capacity to love deeply again.

Grief and love are intricately tied together. Love of our lost ones, love shared among those still with us, sustains us through our grief. Grief shows us the importance of love, helping us to become whole again.

# Tips for Coping

1. Identify what you're feeling.

2. Acknowledge your thoughts and share them with others.

3. Ask for what you need.

4. Believe in yourself.

5. Listen.

6. Set small goals in the beginning.

7. Schedule specific times to do something you like.

8. Reach out to others.

9. Focus on only one thing at a time.

10. Recognize that some days will be better than others.

11. Realize that love isn't enough, but it is very important.

12. Remember to dream.

13. Be kind to yourself and learn to forgive yourself.

14. Hug yourself and others often.

Time does not really heal a broken heart—
it only teaches a person
how to live with it.

*Anonymous*

Like a flower which,
when the time is right,
scatters its seed upon the wind,
so will your sorrow
one day change and
be carried away in its season,
leaving the seeds
of new life and new hope
where once there was pain.

*Anonymous*

Grief never ends, but it changes.
It's a passage, not a place to stay.
The sense of loss must give way
if we're to value the life that was lived.

*Anonymous*

Just as grief preserves the meaningfulness of the past,
it also opens us slowly to a new future.
Grief is a midwife; it lets the journey continue.
Often after a profound and shattering loss,
we think that we will never to be able to live again.
For a while we think that our life is forever diminished.
We may think that to live again and to know
satisfaction again is to abandon the past.
Grief slowly gives us permission to say
yes to life,
to want to live,
to think that we deserve life.

*John C. Raines*

Listening
has the power
to open doors.
It has the power
to affirm
and care,
and ultimately
to heal.

*Anonymous*

We have no right to ask
when sorrow comes,
"Why did this happen to me?"
unless we ask the same question
for every joy that comes our way.

*Philip S. Bernstein*

The mention of my child's name
may bring tears to my eyes,
but it never fails to bring
music to my ears.

If you really are my friend,
let me hear the beautiful music of her name.
It soothes my broken heart
and sings to my soul.

*Anonymous*

We had seen a few people who belonged to this club, but we didn't seem to have anything in common with them. Occasionally, we read stories in the newspaper about new members being initiated into the club, but it didn't seem likely that we would ever join, so we paid no attention.

The price of membership is so dear that we couldn't imagine being a part of the club. We realized in the backs of our minds that people didn't choose to pay the dues and join. It was done for them.

But without our consent, we are now members in this club known as bereaved parents. The cost of membership was the life of our daughter. Like all other members, we have no idea why we were selected for membership, but there is no resigning from it.

We have learned a lot since our membership began. We now understand much about its other members. In fact, we seek to be with them, to have regular get-togethers in order to discuss our membership and try to understand its value.

Acquaintances often try to ignore our membership, pretending that it doesn't exist. They seem to think that makes things easier for us, that we won't feel "different," but it only makes things much worse.

So many times I have wanted someone to say that she thought of my absent child, a part of whom still lives on inside me and overshadows all of my thoughts. Instead I hear friends whisper to each other that they don't want to upset me, or remind me of my daughter, or say something that might make me cry.

Don't they understand that I am thinking of her nearly twenty-four hours a day? The only way to make me feel any worse is to pretend that my beloved child never existed at all.

I need to talk about my child, and it helps me so much to hear others talk about her as well. As much as I never, ever wanted to become a member of this club, the support we offer each, and the ability to share the memories of our loved ones and the lessons they taught us, makes participation in the club essential for so many members. It is one of the ways that we manage to continue on.

*Karen Grover*

There's an elephant in the room.
It is large and squatting,
so it is hard to get around.

Yet, we squeeze by with, "How are you?"
and "I'm fine,"
and a thousand other forms
of trivial chatter.

We talk about the weather.
We talk about work.
We talk about everything else
except the elephant in the room.

We all know it is there.
We are thinking about the elephant as we talk.
It is constantly on our minds,
for it is a very big elephant.

But we do not talk about
the elephant in the room.

Oh, please, say her name.
Oh, please, say "Barbara" again.
Oh, please, let's talk about the elephant
in the room.

For as we talk about her death,
perhaps we can talk about her life.
Can I say "Barbara"
and not have you look away?
For if I cannot, you are leaving me
alone,
in a room
with an elephant.

*Terry Kettering*

When you accept as a simple fact
that I feel what I feel
no matter how irrational,
then I can quit trying to convince you
and get about the business
of understanding myself.

And when that's clear,
the answers will be obvious
and I won't need advice.

*So please listen*
*and just hear me.*

And, if you want to talk,
wait a minute for your turn,
and I will listen to you.

*Ralph Roughton, M.D.*

Grief is neither a sign of weakness
nor a lack of faith.
It is the price we pay
for love.

*Darcie Sims*

# A Bereaved Parent's Wish List

1. I wish my child hadn't died. I wish I had him back.

2. I wish you wouldn't be afraid to speak my child's name. My child lived and was important to me. I need to hear that he was important to you also.

3. If I cry and get emotional when you talk about my child, I want you to know it isn't because you have hurt me. My child's death is the cause of my tears. You have talked about my child, and you have allowed me to share my grief. I thank you for both.

4. I wish you wouldn't kill my child again by removing his pictures, artwork, or other remembrances from your home.

5. Being a bereaved parent is not contagious, so I wish you wouldn't shy away from me. I need you now more than ever.

6. I need diversions, so I do want to hear about you; but I also want you to hear about me. I might be sad and I might cry, but I wish you would let me talk about my child, my favorite topic of the day.

7. I know that you think of and pray for me often. I also know that my child's death pains you, too. I wish you would let me know those things through a phone call, a card, a note, or a big hug.

8. I wish you could understand that my grief will never be over. I will suffer the death of my child until the day I die.

9. I wish you wouldn't expect me not to think about it or to be happy. Neither will happen for a very long time.

10. I wish you understood how my life has shattered. I know it is unpleasant for you to be around me when I'm feeling miserable. Please be as patient with me as you can.

11. When I say, "I'm doing okay," I wish you could understand that I don't feel okay and that I struggle daily.

12. I wish you knew that all of the grief reactions I'm having are normal. Depression, anger, hopelessness, and overwhelming sadness are all to be expected. So please excuse me when I'm quiet and withdrawn or irritable and cranky.

13. Your advice to take one day at a time is excellent. However, a day is too much and too fast for me right now. I wish you could understand that I'm doing well to handle one hour at a time.

14. Please excuse me if I seem rude; that's certainly not my intent. Sometimes the world around me goes too fast and I need to slow things down. When I walk away, I wish you would let me find a quiet place to spend time alone.

15. I wish you understood that grief changes people. When my child died, a big part of me died with him. I am not the same person I was before my child died, and I will never be that person again.

16. I wish very much that you could understand—understand my loss and my grief, my silence and my tears, my void and my pain. But I pray daily that you will never be able to truly understand.

*Diane Collins*

Many people are convinced
that being strong and brave
means trying to think and talk
about something else.
But we know
that being strong and brave
means thinking and talking
about our dead love,
until our grief begins to be bearable.
That is strength;
that is courage.
And only thus can being strong and brave
help you heal.

*Sasha Wagner*

Once there was a little girl who went on an errand for her mother. She was late coming back and her mother asked for an explanation. The child explained that a playmate of hers down the street had fallen and broken her doll, and that she had helped her. The mother wondered what she could do to help mend the broken doll. The little girl made a marvelous reply: "I just sat down and helped her cry." There are times when we cannot solve other people's problems; we can only become part of their grief.

*Charles Allen*

Teach me to laugh again,
but never let me forget I cried.

*Anonymous*

They mean so well when they say:
"You're so strong."
What they really mean is:
"I wouldn't like it if you cried in front of me."

They mean so well when they say:
"How are you?"
What they really mean is:
"How are you since your son died?"

They mean so well when they say:
"You look so well."
What they really mean is:
"I'm glad that you're not wearing your grief today."

I wish I had a little window
so they could look inside my
heart and soul.

Then they wouldn't have to mean so well.

*Deborah Spungen*

Someone asked me about you today.
It's been so long since anyone has done that.

If felt so good to talk about you,
to share my memories of you,
to say your name out loud.

She asked me if I minded talking
about what happened to you
or if it would be too painful
to speak of it.

I told her that I think of it
every day,
and speaking about it
helps me to release
the tormented thoughts
whirling around in my head.
She said she never realized
the pain would last this long.
She apologized for not asking sooner.
I told her, "Thanks for asking."

I don't know if it was curiosity
or concern
that made her ask,
but I told her,
"Please do it again sometime soon."

*Barbara Taylor Hudson*

It's okay to grieve.
The death of a child is devastating.

It's okay to cry.
Tears relieve the pressure of a broken heart.

It's okay to heal.
It's a sign that you have learned to accept death.

It's okay to laugh.
Laughter is not a sign of less grief or less love.

It means you have allowed the happy memories of your
child to take root inside you.

*Linda Anderson*

Grief is a solitary journey. No one but you knows how great the hurt is. No one but you can know the gaping hole left in your life when someone you know has died. And no one but you can hear the silence that was once filled with laughter and song. It is the nature of love and death to touch every person in a totally unique way. And solace comes from understanding how others have learned to sing again.

*Helen Steiner Rice*

There is sacredness in tears.
They are not the mark of weakness,
but of power.

They speak more eloquently
than ten thousand tongues.

They are messengers
of overwhelming grief,
of deep contrition
and of unspeakable love.

*Washington Irving*

I remember going back to work, sitting at my desk and staring blankly at the walls. The people I worked with struggled to say the right things, but they continued, also, to do the same things they always did. I wished or expected or wanted something to be different, because my world had changed so drastically.

I remember seeing my friends again. And they were kind and brought food or said they were sorry, or they hugged me and maybe cried with me. But they were still the same friends, eating the same foods and reading the same books, and I guess I thought they would change, for certainly I had changed since I had last seen them.

And the news on TV and the time of year and the color of the sky and everything else must surely change, but it didn't and it doesn't and the world impossibly, capriciously continues just as it always has.

The death of a child has probably changed each of us more than any single event in our lives. And the world seems cruel sometimes not to allow us the time to adjust and catch up. But no amount of hoping will stop the goings-on around us. Slowly, strongly and eventually we must make the effort, on our own, to catch up.

*Gerald Hunt*

Grieving is a fierce and overwhelming expression of love thrust upon us by a deep and hurtful loss. Yet we often fail to recognize that forgiveness must be an integral part of our grief and our healing.

We learn to forgive our children for dying, and ourselves for not preventing it. We begin to forgive God. We start to forgive relatives and friends for abandoning us in their own bewilderment over the emotions they sense in our words and behavior.

We must be open to the balm of forgiveness. Through its expression in our lives, be it through thought, word or deed, we find small ways to seek life once more. Deep within us, forgiveness can help us feel again the love that has not died.

Let us heed the quiet message heard so softly in the maelstrom of the spirit. Forgive, forgive, and forgive until forever. Let love enfold our anguish, helping us to grow and strive beyond this hour to a rich tomorrow.

*Don Hackett*

Will you forgive me if I go on?
If you can't make this earthly journey
through time with me,
will you, then,
come along in my heart
and wish me well?

*Betty Johnson*

Where there is pain,
let there be softening.

Where there is bitterness,
let there be acceptance.

Where there is silence,
let there be communication.

Where there is loneliness,
let there be friendship.

Where there is despair,
let there be hope.

*Ruth Eiseman*

Grieving as
a Couple

f all the trials that test the bonds of marriage, none is more overwhelming than the death of a child. You are not only two people grieving together, but also two separate, grieving individuals.

A child's death can create emotional distance in couples. Our emotions are raw, and despair and pain surface at different times. It is difficult to sort things out or give much to each other. We often feel alone and wonder if our spouse understands how we are feeling.

People grieve differently. How we feel, when we express emotions, how much we want to talk about the death and our grief, our need for physical contact, and our spiritual thoughts often differ. Some of us need to express ourselves openly and often. For others, grieving takes place mostly in private. These differences can cause misunderstandings and make us feel abandoned.

Express your feelings, or keep them to yourself, but do not blame each other. Be gentle and patient. Move slowly as you begin to heal. Cherish the special memories you made with your child. Always be open to sharing and, most importantly, to listening.

The need to respect your spouse's feelings is one of the most important jobs that you will ever be asked to do. Move cautiously for the first year. Take time to make important decisions; be sensitive to your spouse's needs, and to your own. This will require much love and compassion. As honestly as possible, express your needs with each other. There will be times when you need to be hugged, times when you need to be alone with your grief, and times when you need to talk. Celebrate your relationship when you can; learn to take the risk of loving deeply again. Reach out for each other.

Many of the most intense conflicts couples have are about making sense of the death of their child. Try not to plague yourself with too many "whys" and "what ifs." It is a road you do not want to take, because it leads nowhere. It is important to acknowledge any problems you had in your relationship with your child, but then put them to rest—because no matter what you try to do or figure out, it will not bring your child back.

The search for the meaning of your child's death will not be found in the life lost, but in your own commitment to life.

After a long while, you will learn to love and admire the strength and perseverance of your spouse, knowing that they had as difficult a path to walk as you. The pain of loss will still be there, but you will have added a new dimension to your partnership, and you can share the happy memories of your child for the rest of your lives.

The ultimate test of a relationship is to disagree but to hold hands.

*Alexandra Penney*

Never forget what you lost.
Learn to value what you have.

*Anonymous*

Reach for your spouse's hand.
Be open to your differences.
Be a good listener.
Appreciate silence.
Support your spouse at all times.
Be sensitive to your vulnerability
and the tendency to take things too seriously.
Try not to put unrealistic demands on yourself or your spouse.
Be good to yourself.
Lower your expectations, for now.
Exercise.
Eat well.
Get lots of rest.
Do not isolate yourself.
Grieving the loss of a child will be the hardest work you will ever do.

*Linda Anderson*

We created you
with our love.

We cared for you
with our love.

We nurtured you
with our love.

We honored you
with our love.

We buried you
with our love,

We remember you
with our love.

*Alice and Otto Weening*

When a child dies, grief is a family affair.
It hits Mom and Dad and siblings with equal despair.

Mom cries and cannot get out of bed.
Dad holds emotions and leaves much unsaid.

Sisters and brothers simply cannot understand
Why death came and dealt this kind of hand.

No one acts as they should and nothing is the same.
The family wants to draw together but seems to share only pain.

Someone must be responsible when a child dies.
Each family member thinks in some way it's them, and cries.

But no one is responsible for things we cannot control.
So reach out to each other and keep the family whole.

Don't let the differences in how you grieve
Change the love in your family or its beliefs.

Be strong when you can and weak when you must.
Love each other with kindness and trust.

For we who have been there and made it through together,
Can say that holding on to each other makes love last forever.

*McMinnville, TCF*

Faith

egardless of your religious affiliation, you will wonder how a loving God could possibly allow the death of your child. This is normal and natural.

God knows the pain in our hearts and gives us the strength to endure all things. Faith does not erase the pain or devastation of the loss of our child, but it helps makes it bearable.

In the beginning, we are angry and cannot imagine any good thing that could come from our child's death. But as we continue down the path to healing, we find that we are a little bit wiser and a great deal stronger. When we feel helpless, we often turn to a spiritual source of strength. We can connect with that source and rely on its power to find peace and new meaning in our lives.

In the depth of our loss, we discover that we look differently on life and death. We no longer function in our own little worlds, and we reach out to others in a much more compassionate way. We listen more and talk less. We feel more deeply than we did before we became acquainted with grief. Because of our own trials, we now know how to comfort others.

God is ever present to renew our strength and encourage us. God loves us unconditionally, just as we are right now. God knows our hearts and desires comfort and peace for us.

When the righteous cry for help, the Lord hears,
and rescues them from all their troubles.

The Lord is near to the brokenhearted,
and saves the crushed in spirit.

*Psalm 34:17-18*

I asked God to grant me patience.
God said, No.
Patience is a byproduct of tribulation;
it isn't granted, it is learned.

I asked God to spare me pain.
God said, No.
Suffering draws you apart from worldly cares
and brings you closer to me.

I asked God to make my spirit grow.
God said, No.
You must grow on your own, but I will
prune you to make you fruitful.

I asked God for all things that I might enjoy all things.
God said, No.
I will give you life, so that you may enjoy all things.

I asked God to help me love others
as much as He loves me.
God said, Ahhh, finally you have the idea!

*Anonymous*

If you stand very still in the heart
of the wood you will hear many
wonderful things…

The snap of a twig and the wind in
the trees and the whir of invisible
wings…

If you stand very still in the
turmoil of life and you wait for
the voice from within…

You'll be led down the quiet way of
wisdom and peace—in a mad world
of chaos and din…

If you stand very still and you hold
to your faith—you will get all the
help that you ask…

You will draw from the Silence the
things that you need—hope and
courage, and strength for your task.

*Patience Strong*

I have in my hands two boxes
which God gave me to hold.
He said, "Put all your sorrows in the black.
and all your joys in the gold."

I heeded His words, and in the two boxes
both my joys and sorrow I stored.
But though the gold became heavier each day
the black was as light as before.

With curiosity, I opened the black.
I wanted to find out why.
And I saw, in the base of the box, a hole
which my sorrow had fallen out by.

I showed the hole to God, and mused aloud,
"I wonder where my sorrows could be."
He smiled a gentle smile at me.
"My child, they're all here with me."

I asked, "God, why give me the boxes.
why the gold, and the black with the hole?"
"My child, the gold is for you to count your blessings,
the black is for you to let go."

*Anonymous*

Lord, I wonder:
do you permit grief that I might learn
to be content with nothing less
that the comfort of God?
Whatever the reason,
one thing I am learning:
You make useful to me
all that you permit.
So, dear God,
though a great ache wells within my heart,
I ask you to grip my life.
Help me to bring Your comfort to others
As you are now comforting me.

*Ruth Harms Calkin*

A baby is a small miracle,
God's way of saying He wants the world to continue.
As children, we nurture you and prepare you to be presented
to the world as good men and women.
We hope to give you roots,
then wings to develop your own self,
find a mate, and continue the cycle.
We have hopes and dreams for each child.
Raising children is a mixture of pain,
joy, disappointment and happiness.
We expect to diminish as our children grow and mature.
When God calls our children home before us,
we are saddened beyond words or expression,
because we miss them in our lives.
But we continue to live and love life
and trust in God's plan for all of us.
What we see dimly now,
we shall see fully in heaven.

*Anonymous*

To let go is to admit powerlessness,
which means the outcome is not in my hands.

To let go is not to try to change or blame another,
it is to make the most of myself.

To let go is not to care for,
but to care about.

To let go is not to fix,
but to be supportive.

To let go is not to judge,
but to allow another to be a human being.

To let go is not to be in the middle,
arranging all the outcomes,
but to allow God to work His will in the lives of others.

To let go is not to be protective,
it is to permit another to face reality.

To let go is not to deny,
but to accept.

To let go is not to nag, scold or argue,
but instead to search out my own shortcomings
and allow God to correct them.

To let go does not mean to deny the shortcomings of others,
but to accept others unconditionally in love.

To let go is not to adjust everything to my desires,
but to accept each day as it comes,
knowing God offers it to me for growth.

To let go is not to criticize or regulate anybody,
but to try to become what I understand
God wants me to be.

To let go does not mean to compete against another human being,
but to compete within myself to learn self-control
through circumstances God brings into my life.

To let go means I don't demand my own way,
but that I hold firm to my values and beliefs,
while allowing others the same privilege.

To let go doesn't mean that I expect God to do everything for me,
but that I let Him show me how to do His will in my life.

*Anonymous*

When we do the best we can
we never know
what miracle is wrought
in our life,
or
in the life of another.

*Helen Keller*

Memories

mmediately after the death of our child, we may not want to think back on the times we shared with them. It may be too painful to feel much of anything, and we will try to protect ourselves from the pain of our loss. This is normal and natural.

Eventually, though, the good memories will come back and you will treasure the recollections of your child in those happy times. These memories will keep you close to them and will help to bridge the past with the present.

Memories can be a positive part of healing as you acknowledge that your child would want you to be happy again and live a productive life, even without their presence.

As you heal, you may recall the not-so-happy times as well as the happy ones, but these memories are equally important. Your remaining family must know that you are grieving, but also that you do not pretend that your child was perfect. Allow yourself to remember your child as they were, not as you wished them to be—and then, have a forgiving heart.

I put my own special memories in a box, ready to open whenever I feel empty and need to feel my child's love. I still carry my daughter's picture in my billfold. Once in a while, I see someone who looks like her, and I smile.

Memories are worth keeping.

∽

Time cannot steal the treasure
that we carry in our hearts,
nor ever dim the shining thought
our cherished past imparts,
for memories of the one we loved
still cast a gentle glow
to grace our days and light our paths
wherever we may go.

*Anonymous*

There is a place
that we call Memory—
a province by itself,
which though unseen
is home and haven
to the heart—
and there,
in peace and beauty,
waiting,
are those with whom
we shared our yesterdays.

*Nancy Cassell*

In the rising of the sun and in its going down,
we remember them;
In the blowing of the wind and in the chill of the winter,
we remember them;
In the opening of buds and in the rebirth of spring,
we remember them;
In the warmth of the sun and the peace of summer,
we remember them;
In the rustling of the leaves and the beauty of autumn,
we remember them;
In the beginning of the year and when it ends,
we remember them;

When we are weary and in the need of strength,
we remember them;
When we are lost and sick at heart,
we remember them;
When we have joys we yearn to share,
we remember them;
So long as we live, they too shall live,
for they are now a part of us,
as we remember them.

*Anonymous*

We can't know why the lily has so brief
a time to bloom in the warmth of
sunlight's kiss upon its face
before it folds its fragrance in and bids
the world goodnight to rest its
beauty in a gentler place.

But we can know that nothing that is
loved is ever lost, and no one who
has ever touched a heart can
really pass away, because some
beauty lingers on in each memory
of which they've been a part.

*Ellen Brennerman*

Sometimes,
memories are like shadows,
sneaking up behind you,
following you around—
then they disappear
leaving you sad and confused.

Sometimes,
memories are like comforters,
surrounding you with warmth,
luxuriously abundant—
and sometimes they stay,
wrapping you in contentment.

*Marcia Updyke*

I am fooling only myself when
I say my daughter exists now
only in the photograph on my bulletin board
or in the outline of my hand
or in the armful of memories
I still hold tight.
She lives on beneath everything I do.
Her presence influences who I was
and her absence influences who I am.
Our lives are shaped as much by those who leave
as they are by those who stay.
Loss is our legacy,
insight our gift.
Memory is our guide.

*Marion Hope Edelman*

In one of the stars I shall be living.
In one of them I shall be laughing.
And so it will be as if all the stars were laughing
when you look at the sky at night.

And there is sweetness in the laughter of all the stars
and in the memories of those you love.

*Antoine DeSaint-Exupery*

Right now
take a moment
close your eyes
and remember
the smile
of your child.

*Sasha Wagner*

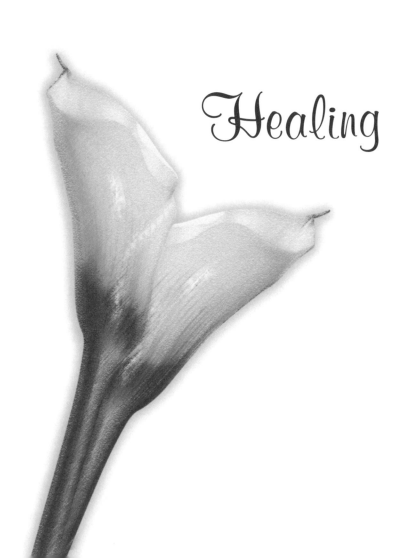

Healing

he difference between recovery and healing is that in healing we do not return to who we were, but become a new version of ourselves, integrating our loss into who we have become. We are not just putting our lives back together—we are creating new lives for ourselves.

We have to accept what we cannot change, find new meaning in our lives, accept our limitations and use our experience to become more loving, patient and giving.

Our feelings of loss may never end, but going through the valley of grief has led us to a deeper commitment to others and to God. We have become better listeners, able to share our pain and feel the pain of others. In a sense, we have become the prophets of the belief that God will never shut a door without also opening a window.

We determine the meaning in our lives, our sense of purpose, and the amount of happiness we allow ourselves. The choice to live life to the fullest, in spite of our loss, is a conscious decision that we make.

Peace comes when we accept the death of our child. May you be granted peace and healing in your life, and may you always treasure the memories of your beloved child.

Hope is not pretending that troubles don't exist.
It is the trust that they will not last forever,
that hurts will be healed
and difficulties overcome.
It is faith,
a source of strength and renewal.
that lies within,
to lead us through the dark
to the sunshine.

*Anonymous*

Will I ever be happy again?
Yes, but it will be a different
kind of happiness,
neither better or worse,
just different.
Relax into it and see what happens.

*Darcie Sims*

Just for today I will adjust myself to what is. I will face reality. I will connect those things that I can and accept those things I cannot correct.

Just for today I will live through this day only, and not set far-reaching goals to try to overcome all my problems at once. I know I can do something for twenty-four hours that would overwhelm me if I thought I had to keep it up for a lifetime.

Just for today I will gather the courage to do what is right and take responsibility for my own actions.

*Anonymous*

The clock of time is wound just once
and no man has the power
to tell just when the hands will stop
on what day or what hour.

Now is the only time you have
so live it with a will—
don't wait until tomorrow,
the hands may then be still.

*Anonymous*

Come, take my hand; the road is long. We must travel by stepping stones.

No, you are not alone. I'll be with you. I know the road well; I've been there.

We must take one step at a time and we may have to stop awhile. It is a long way to the other side and there are many obstacles.

We have many stones to cross. Some are bigger than others—shock, denial and anger, to start. Then come guilt, despair and loneliness. It's a hard road to travel, but it must be done. It's the only way to the other side.

Come, slip your hand in mine. It's strong. I've held so many hands like yours. Yes, mine was once small and weak, too. Once, I also had to take someone's hand in order to take the first step.

Oops! You've stumbled; go ahead and cry. Don't be ashamed; I understand. Let's wait here awhile so you can get your breath. When you're stronger we'll go on, one step at a time. There's no need to hurry.

Say, it's nice to hear you laugh. Yes, I agree, the memories you shared are good.

Look, we're halfway there now. I can see the other side. Its looks so warm and sunny.

Oh, look, we're nearing the last stone and you're standing alone. And look, your hand—you've let go of mine. We've reached the other side.

But wait, look back. Someone is standing there. They are alone and want to cross the stepping stones. I'd better go, they need my help.

What? Are you sure? Why, yes, go ahead. I'll wait. You know the way; you've been there.

Yes, I agree, it's your turn, my friend, to help someone else cross the stepping stones.

*Barbara Williams*

I never believed I would see another season
change with gladness.

I never believed I would see the world again
without the haze of tears.

I never expected to actually laugh again.
I never felt my smile would return and feel
natural on my face.

I never hoped for another day when
I would not want to die.

I never envisioned a world that could
again be bright and full of promise.

I believed that all that had passed from me
the day our child died would never return.

But I was wrong.
And I know that in the fullness of your grieving
you, too, will come to understand that life goes on—
that it can still have meaning—
that even joy can touch your life once more.

*Don Hackett*

Am I healing?

I'm able to gaze at her photograph without that
tourniquet tightening around my throat,
claiming memory.

I'm beginning to see her in her life,
and not only myself bereft of her life.

Piece by piece,
I re-enter the world.

A new phase,
a new body,
a new voice.

Birds console me by flying,
trees by growing,
dogs by the warm patch they leave
behind on the sofa,
unknown people merely by
performing their motions.

It's like a slow recovery from a sickness,
this recovery of one's self.

*Tony Talbot*

*Be there for me:*
I feel alone, in pain.
I need a special friend

*Share my sorrow:*
Speak from your heart.
I have to talk about my feelings.

*Let me grieve:*
Listen to me, I need to cry.
We all grieve in our own way and in a different time frame.

*Keep the memory alive:*
It is always on my mind.
I have so many memories.

*I need your help:*
Help me, call me, pray for me.
Do whatever you can.

*Don't desert me:*
Don't desert me after the first or second week.
I need you especially on holidays.

*Take care of yourself:*
I need to depend on you.

*Help me to heal:*
Involve me, listen to me months later.
I need your interest and invitations.

*Be my friend:*
Don't be afraid of me or my grief.
It's okay to cry.
Lastly, please don't criticize me until you've walked in my shoes.

*Instead:*
Pray for me.

*Anonymous*

I don't know why…
I'll never know why…
I don't have to know why…
I don't have to like it….
What I have to do is make a choice about my living.
What I want to do is accept it and go on living.
The choice is mine.
I can go on living,
valuing every moment in a way I
never did before.
Or, I can be destroyed by it
and, in turn, destroy others.
I thought I was immortal,
that my children and family were also,
that tragedy happened only to others…
But I know now that life is tenuous and valuable.
And I choose to go on living,
making the most of the time I have,
and valuing my family and friends
in a way I never experienced before.

*Iris Bolton*

The longer I live, the more I realize the impact of attitude on life. Attitude, to me, is more important than facts. It is more important than the past, than education, than money, than circumstances, than failures, than success, than what other people think or say or do. It is more important than appearance, giftedness or skill. It will make or break a company...a church...a home. The remarkable thing is we have a choice every day regarding the attitude we will embrace for that day. We cannot change the inevitable. The only thing we can do is play on the one string we have, and that is our attitude. I am convinced that ten percent of life is what happens to me and ninety percent is how I react to it...

*Anonymous*

A stream was working itself across the country, experiencing little difficulty. It ran around the rocks and through the mountains.

Then it arrived at a desert. Just as it had crossed every other barrier, the stream tried to cross this one, but it found that as fast as it ran into the sand, its waters disappeared. It appeared that there was no way it could continue the journey.

Then a voice came in the wind. "If you stay the way you are you cannot cross the sands; you cannot become more than a quagmire. To go further you will have to lose yourself."

"But if I lose myself," the stream cried, "I will never know what I'm supposed to be."

"Oh, on the contrary," said the voice. "If you lose yourself you will become more than you ever dreamed you could be."

So, the stream surrendered to the sun. And the clouds into which it was formed were carried by the raging wind for many miles. Once it crossed the desert, the stream poured down from the skies, fresh and clean and full of energy from the storm.

*As told by Idries Shah*

Cherish your visions and your dreams,
as they are the children of your soul;
the blueprints
of your ultimate achievements.

*Napoleon Hill*

I do not know what the future holds
of joy or pain,
of loss or gain,
along life's untrod way;
but I believe
I can receive
God's promised guidance day by day;
so I securely travel on.
And if at times the journey leads
through waters deep,
or mountains steep,
I know this unseen Friend,
His love revealing
His presence healing,
walks with me to the journey's end;
so I securely travel on.

*Anonymous*

There are two days in every week that we should not worry about, two days that should be kept free from fear and apprehension.

One is yesterday, with its mistakes and cares, its faults and blunders, its aches and pains. Yesterday has passed, forever beyond our control.

All the money in the world cannot bring back yesterday. We cannot undo a single act we performed or experienced. Nor can we erase a single word we've said or heard. Yesterday is gone.

The other day we shouldn't worry about is tomorrow, with its impossible adversaries, its burden, its hopeful promise and poor performance. Tomorrow is beyond our control.

Tomorrow's sun will rise either in splendor or behind a mask of clouds— but it will rise. And until it does, we have no stake in tomorrow, for it is yet unborn.

This leaves only one day: today. Any person can fight the battles of just one day. It is only when we add the burdens of yesterday and tomorrow that we break down.

It is not the experience of today that drives people mad—it is the remorse or bitterness for something that happened yesterday, and the dread of what tomorrow may bring.

Let us, therefore, live one day at a time.

*Anonymous*

The secret of life isn't in what happens to you, but what you do with what happens to you.

Help other people to cope with their problems and your own will be easier to cope with.

Never use the word impossible again. Toss it into the verbal wastebasket.

Self-trust is the first secret of success. So believe in and trust yourself.

Stand up to your obstacles and do something about them. You will find that they haven't half the strength you think they have.

*Norman Vincent Peale*

Happiness isn't about what happens to us—it's about how we perceive what happens to us. It's the knack of finding a positive for every negative, and viewing a setback as a challenge. It's not wishing for what we don't have, but enjoying what we do possess.

*Lynn Peters*

We cannot change the past.
Our business is to
make ourselves better
and others happy,
and
that is enough
to keep us busy.

*Joseph Fort Newton*

Time is fleeting.
Time is precious.
Take these moments to tell people
you love them
and realize
how precious life can be.
Value today
for we never know
if there will be
a tomorrow.
Don't wait until tomorrow
to tell someone
you love them.

*Francine Rachel Lester*

Tomorrow is not promised, nor is today.
So I choose to celebrate every day I'm alive
by being present in it.

Living in the moment means letting go of
the past and not waiting for the future.

It means living your life consciously, aware
each moment you breathe is a gift.

*Oprah Winfrey*

Each day is made special
by what we can give it,
by how we accept it,
then how we live it.

*Anonymous*

Most of us are uncomfortable thinking of ourselves as artists, but each of us is an artist. With every choice, every day, you are creating a unique work of art, something that only you can do.

The reason you were born was to leave your own indelible mark on the world. This is your authenticity.

Respect your creative urges. Step out in faith and you will discover your choices are as authentic as you are. What is more, you will discover that your life is all it was meant to be: a joyous sonnet of thanksgiving.

*Sarah Ban Breathnack*

We can choose to live and to live fully, or we can let life slip away in a series of missed opportunities.

Meaning is not something you stumble across, like the answer to a riddle or the prize in a treasure hunt. Meaning is something you build into your life. You build it out of your own past, out of your affections and loyalties, out of the experience of humankind as it is passed on to you, out of your own talent and understanding, out of the things you believe in, out of the things and people you love, out of the values for which you are willing to sacrifice something. The ingredients are there. You are the only one who can put them together into a pattern that will be your life. Let it be a life that has dignity and meaning for you. If it does, then the particular balance of success or failure is of less account.

*John Gardner*

The happiest person
is the one who knows
what to remember in the past,
wants to enjoy the present,
and plans for the future.

*Anonymous*

Your Life
to Come

econciling ourselves to the loss of a child takes time and courage. No one else may recognize the effort you have made, yet your experience has made you a more compassionate person who accepts the past, but is very much alive in the present.

Now, with renewed confidence in yourself, you can look forward to a deeper appreciation of life and the ability to give much more to others. There are so many people in the world who need you in their lives. Remember that through our adversity God has taught us three things: we are better able to comfort others because of our experience; we have become thankful for all things; and we are more aware of our dependence on God's guidance.

God will bring people into your life who will be a blessing to you, and you will be a blessing to them. I hope that you will feel as I do and want to do as much good as you can, for all the people you can, for as long as you can. May you be guided by love in all you do.

∽

What lies behind us
and what lies before us
are small matters
compared to
what lies within us.

*Ralph Waldo Emerson*

He proved to me that life truly is fragile, and I will handle it now more carefully.

He taught me that not all problems in life are monumental, and that I must remember to put things in perspective.

He allowed me to reassess my spiritual beliefs. I need to do this from time to time in my life, and that is all right because there is a loving and caring God, who is with me no matter what.

He showed me that each individual, in some way, leaves a mark in this world, or moves someone just so, regardless of how long his life is, or how short.

He gave me a reason and a need to help other people.

He reminded me to show and tell the people I love how I feel about them as often and as openly as I can.

*Linda Worth*

Over time, we learn…
Who is willing to go with us on our grief journey
Who loves us enough to stand by us in good times or bad
To appreciate everyone and everything that helped us heal
To look at our lives and sort out what is important
To find greater meaning in our lives
To love deeply even if we have to say goodbye again
How valuable one life can be.

*Linda Anderson*

The mystery of pain and suffering
can only be answered with
a life that refuses to despair,
refuses to hand one more victory
to the forces of *no*,
but instead makes itself
an instrument of *yes*,
gives itself in love
and compassion
to alleviate pain and suffering.

*Edna Hong*

We don't know
who we are
until
we see
what
we can do.

*Martha Grimes*

Blessed is the influence
of one true,
loving human soul
on another.

*George Eliot*

# The Compassionate Friends
## Contributors

Charles Allen
Karen Berry
Nancy Cassell
Diane Collins
Marian Hope Edelman
Patti Jo Foye
Karen Grover
Don Hackett
Barbara Taylor Hudson
Gerald Hunt
Betty Johnson
John C. Raines
Darcie Sims
Deborah Spungen
Marcia Updyke
Sasha Wagner
Barbara Williams
Linda Worth

# Acknowledgments

I want to thank my husband, Scott, who supported me and encouraged the writing of this book. I am so grateful that you and I were able to pick up the pieces of our lives and discover deep joy and love for each other. As Robert Browning wrote: "Come, grow old with me the best is yet to be!"

To my daughter Heidi, thank you for all the love you so generously share with me. Your beautiful spirit inspires me to be all that I can be.

To my son, Mark, thank you for your silent encouragement.

To my mother, thank you for all the wisdom you have shared with me over the years, your beautiful faith, and your steadfast wish for my happiness.

To my many friends, thank you for comforting me so often and for so long. I wish that I could name all of you. You have allowed me to weep and you have rejoiced when I was able to smile and find joy in life again. I cherish all the things you have done for me.

Thank you, God, for your many blessings and your sustaining comfort each day. There must have been times when you tired of seeing my tears, but you saw my broken heart and continued to lift me up. Thank you for your great love, peace and promise.

Thank you, Sally, for twenty-five years of your life. You were a joy and a blessing in our lives. You left a lasting imprint on many, especially your family.

Last, but certainly not least, thank you, Scott Edelstein, who as my literary agent held a clear vision of this book. Though I struggled through the many re-writes, his vision proved ultimately correct, and for that I am deeply indebted. Your expertise, guidance and direction allowed me to hope that my words could be published and that I could help other bereaved parents envision healing.